World of If

"Spoke of the wind" was originally published in *Quiet Mountain Essays*, Volume VII, Number II, 2009. Used with permission.

Cover art by Boyd McPeek

All artwork is computer generated from original hand drawings.

First Edition 2010
Second Edition 2012
Poem page 34 revised to original draft.

Surfpea Publishing
P.O. Box 46
Sioux Falls, SD 57101
scurfpeapublishing.com
editor@scurfpeapublishing.com

artwork by Boyd McPeek

poems by Charles Luden

World of If

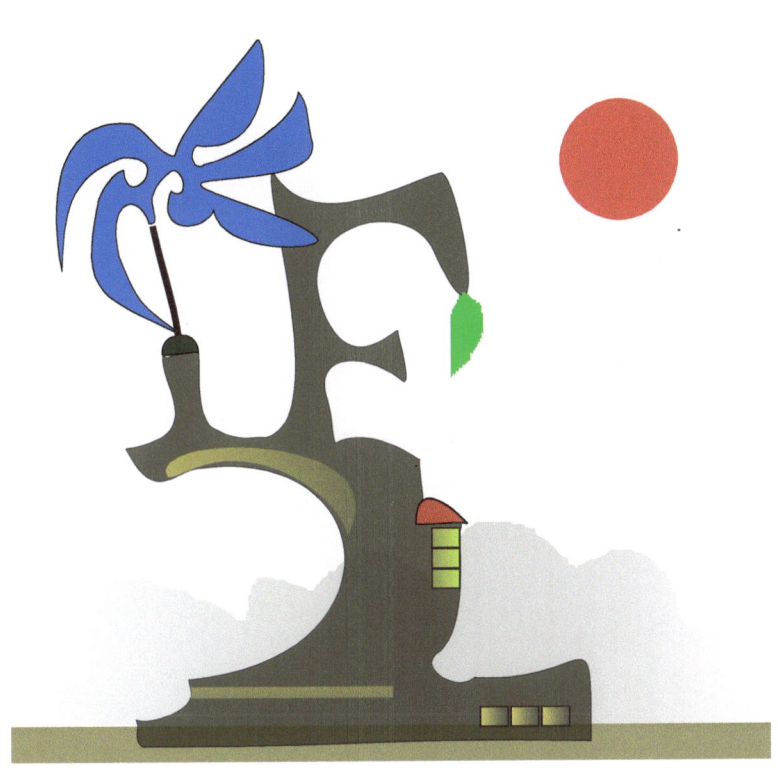

Scurfpea Publishing
Sioux Falls, SD
2010

Contents

World of If

I moved from the city
to the country of the mind.

What do you think about
violations of the soul?

How many transgressions
do the transgressed have?

I heard the phone ring,
and was disappointed.

I did not answer the questions
with reality in my heart.

Sure, I know you.
Will that help me in my life?

Each day I add to my memories,
then I wake up.

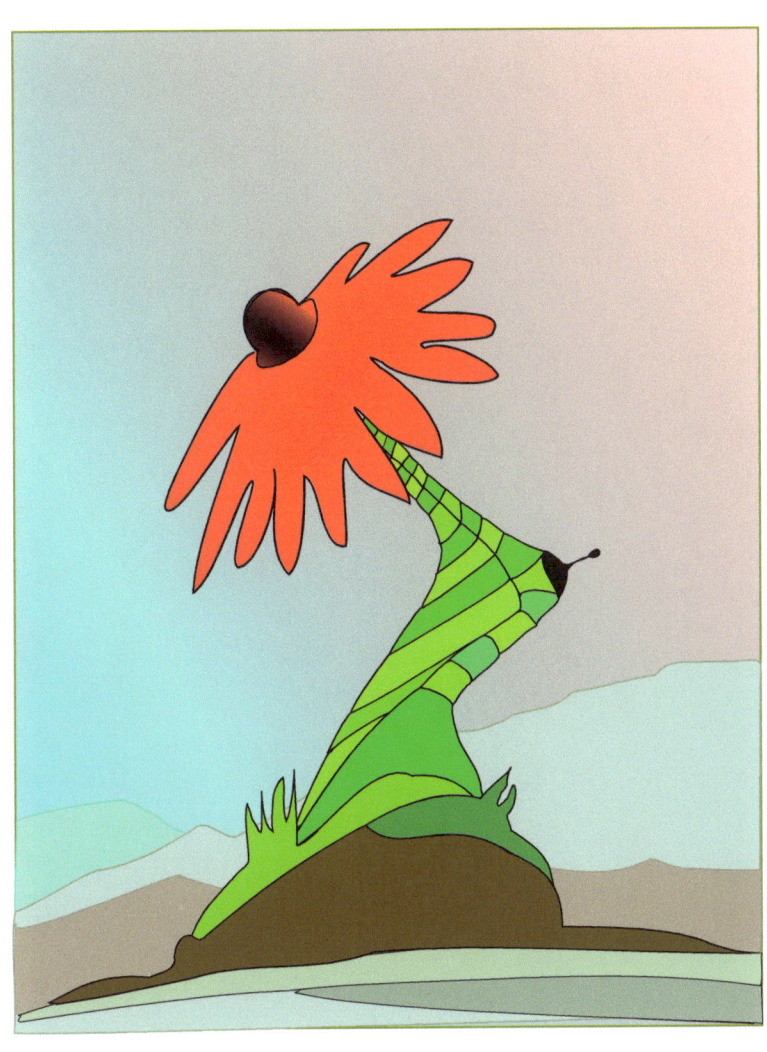

Was here
Guess you weren't
A cloud out the window
is all I remember

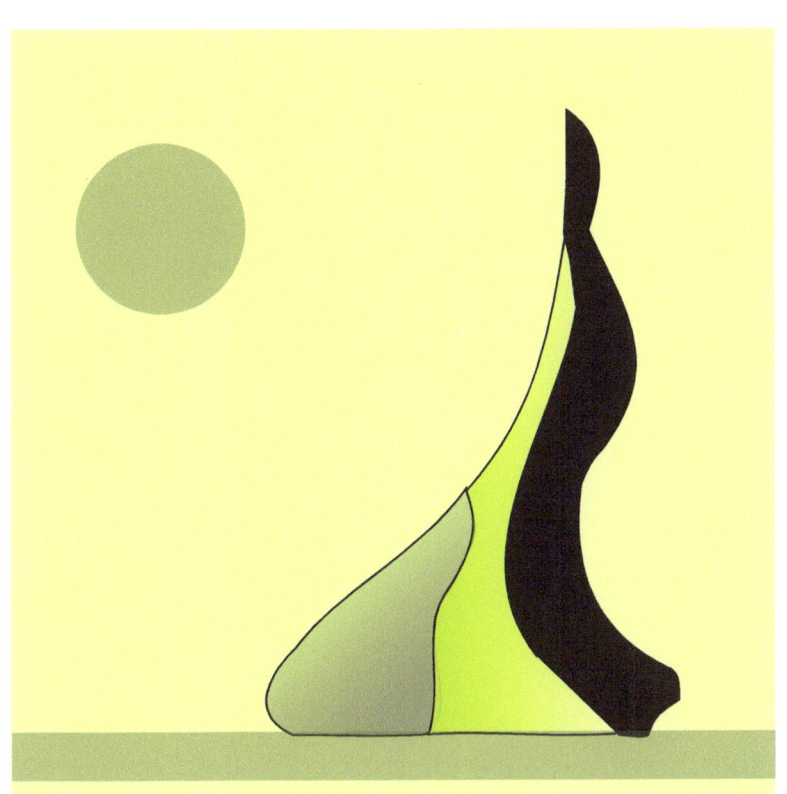

I want to talk about pigeons

I want to talk about death

I want to talk about the stuff
        of the universe

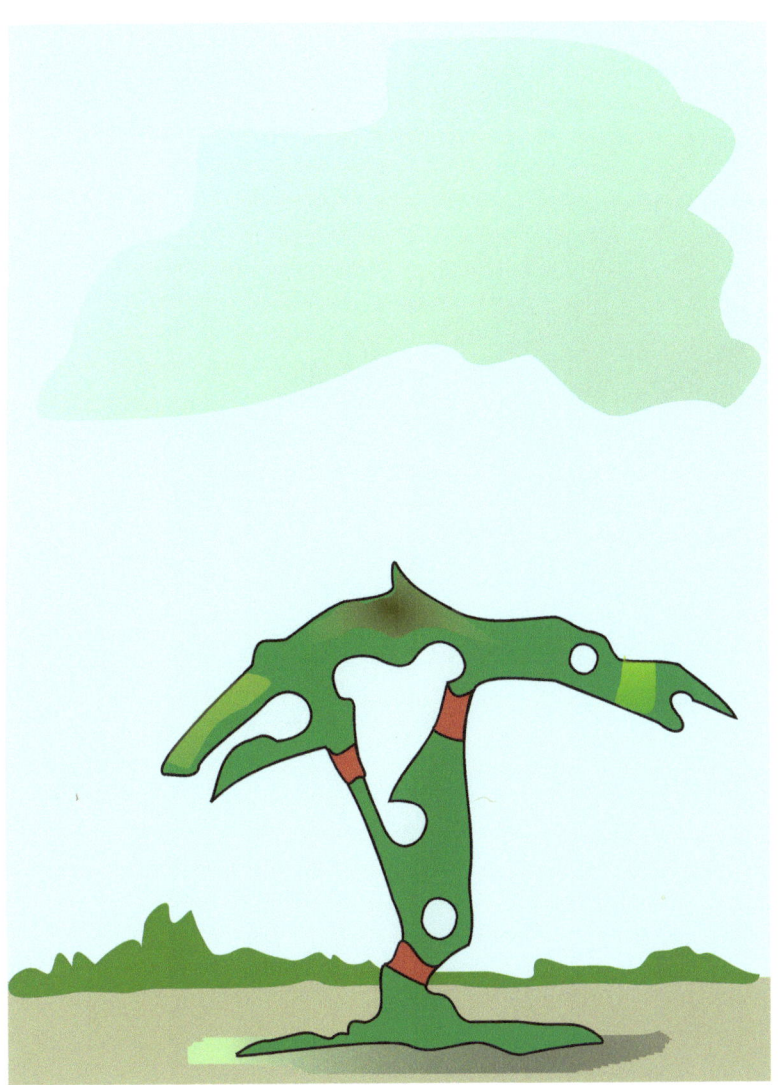

The day
The time
Which never stops
Never begins
Yet
Is always there

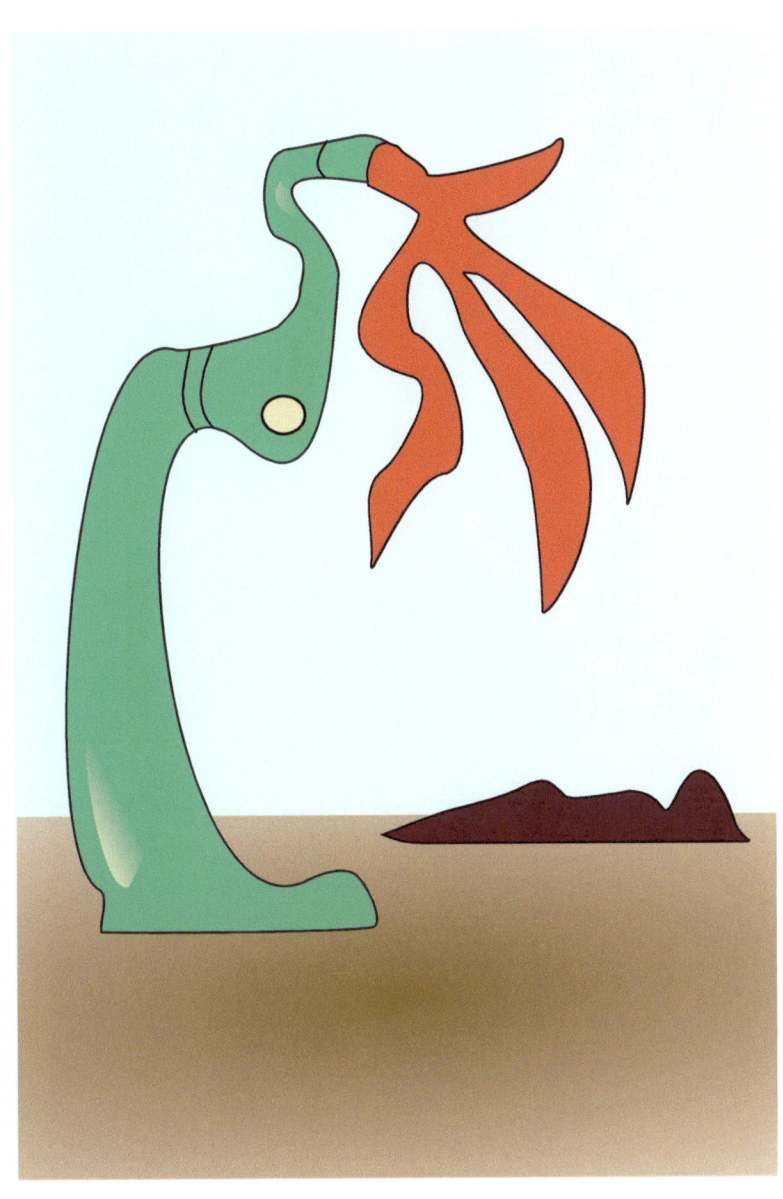

She Looks West

On the horizon fog
On her face mist
On her mind mystery

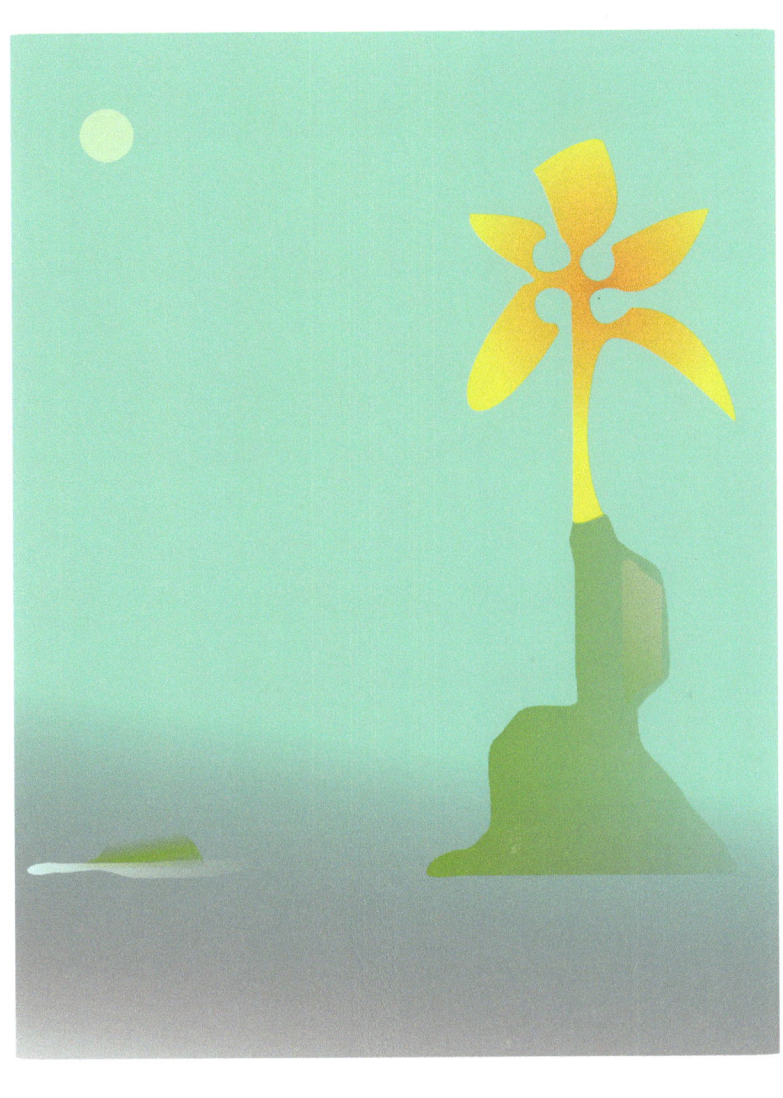

Running Errands for the Soul

The darkness does not interfere
The distance irrelevant
The hole in the horizon
A guide to never being alone

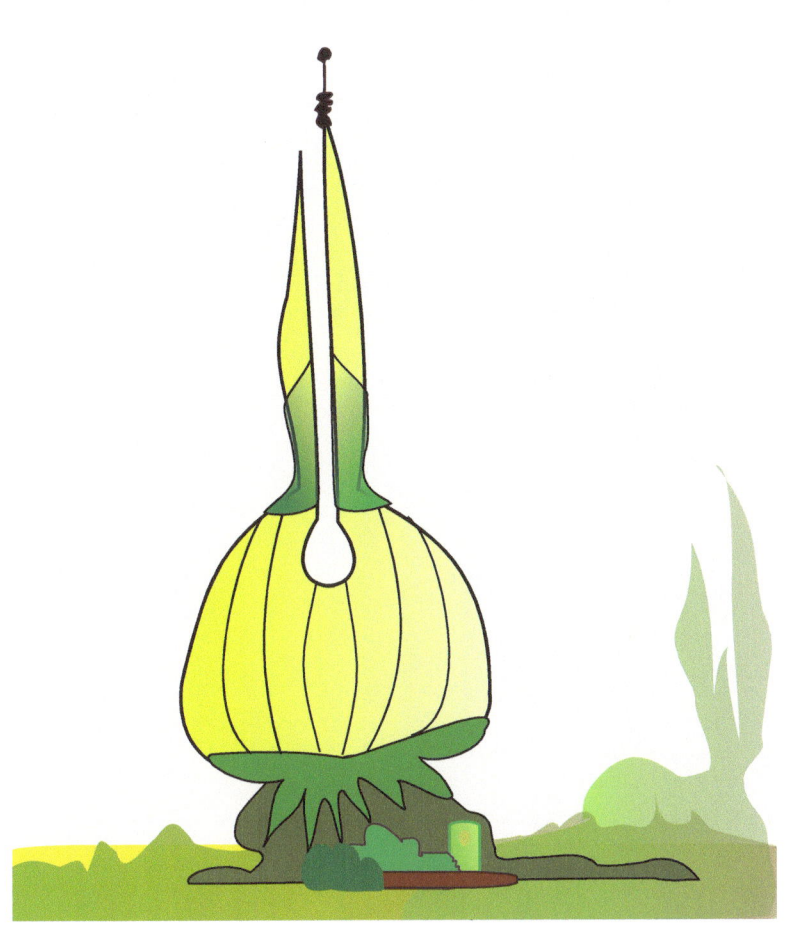

Last Day at the Farm

The wind
Chilly sunny
Many dandelions
A few lady bugs
On the windows
Coffee getting cold
Unknown visitors arrive

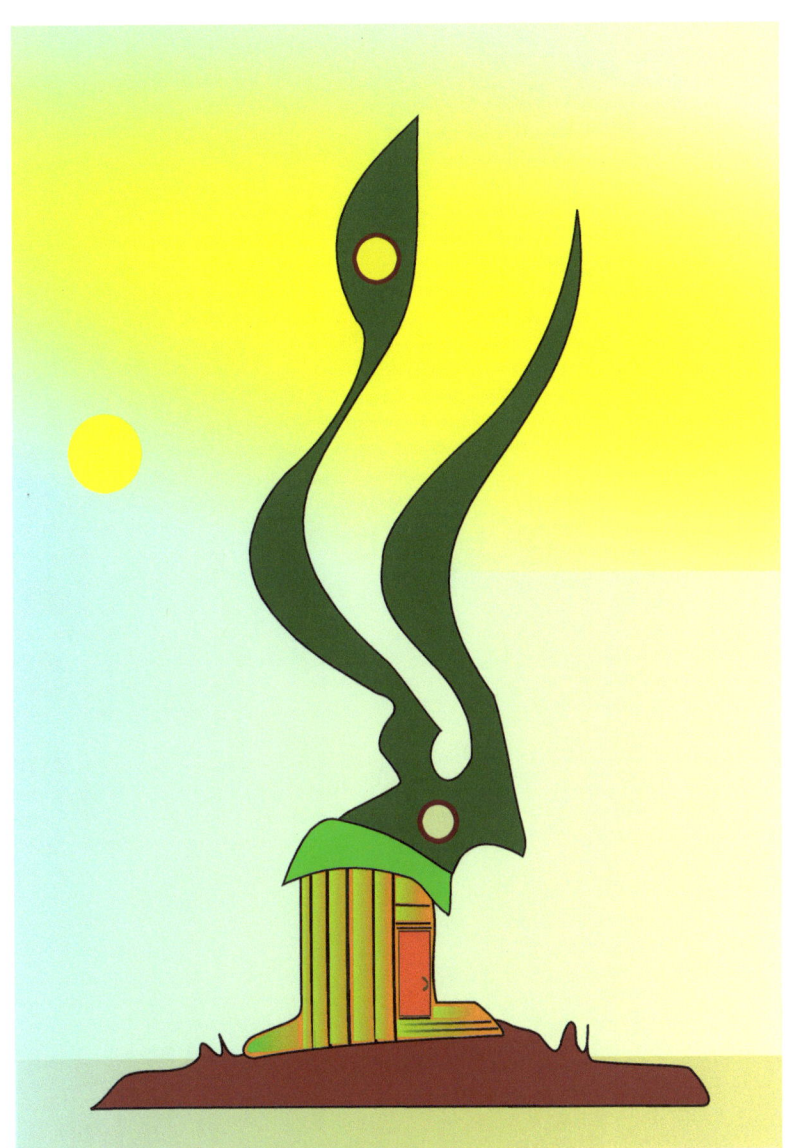

Promise / Memory

The year begins.
Nothing to report
except
her image lingers.

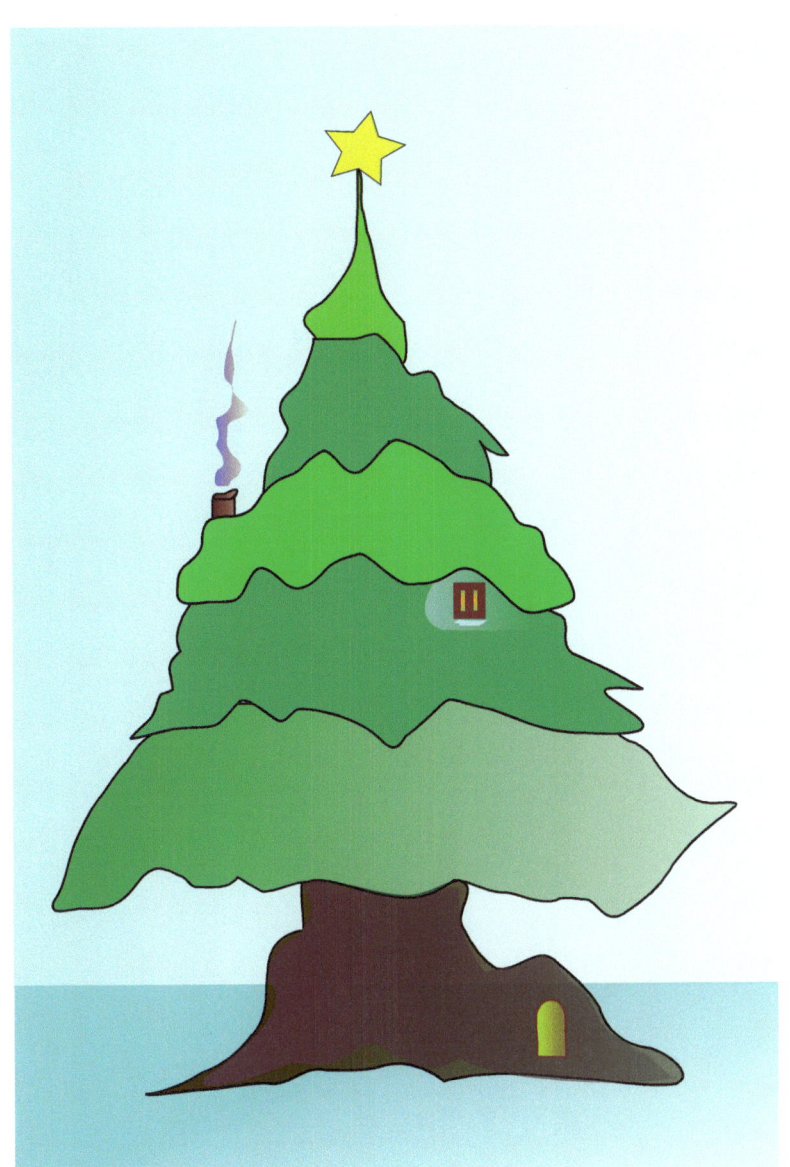

Clear

Perhaps
   magnification is
       the
    answer

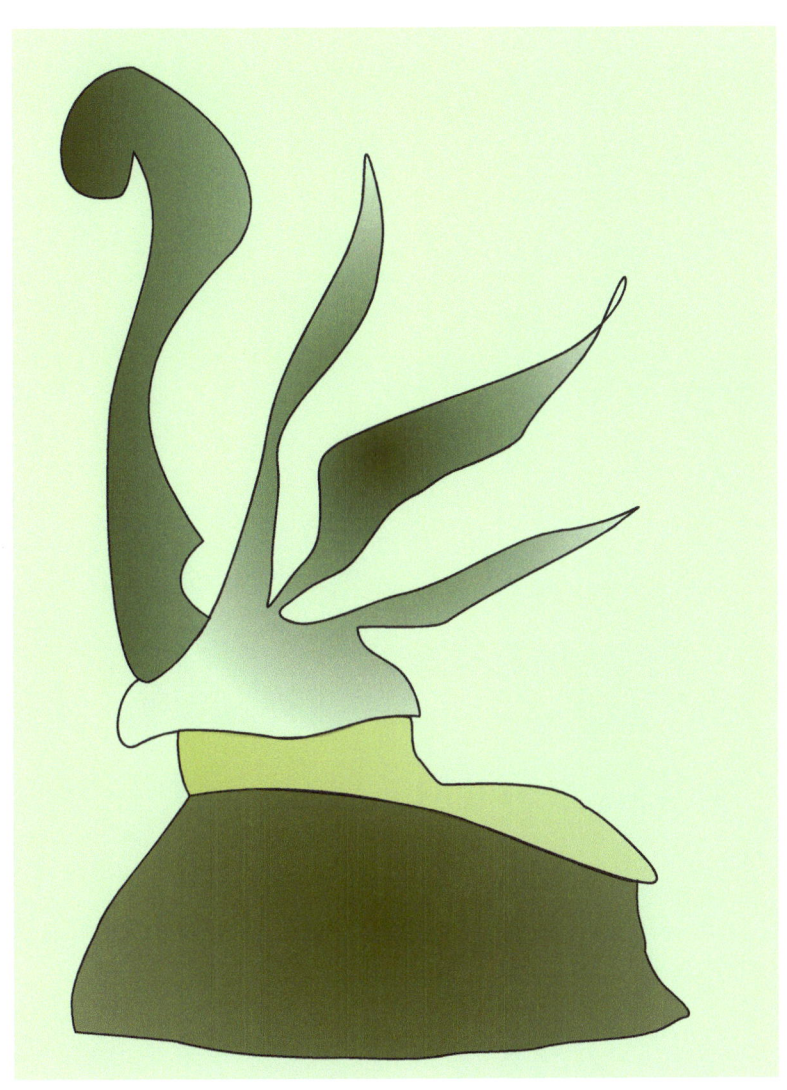

When a bird dies in your hand
does its soul pass through yours
on the way to Heaven?
Your hand, its last tender bed,
closes.

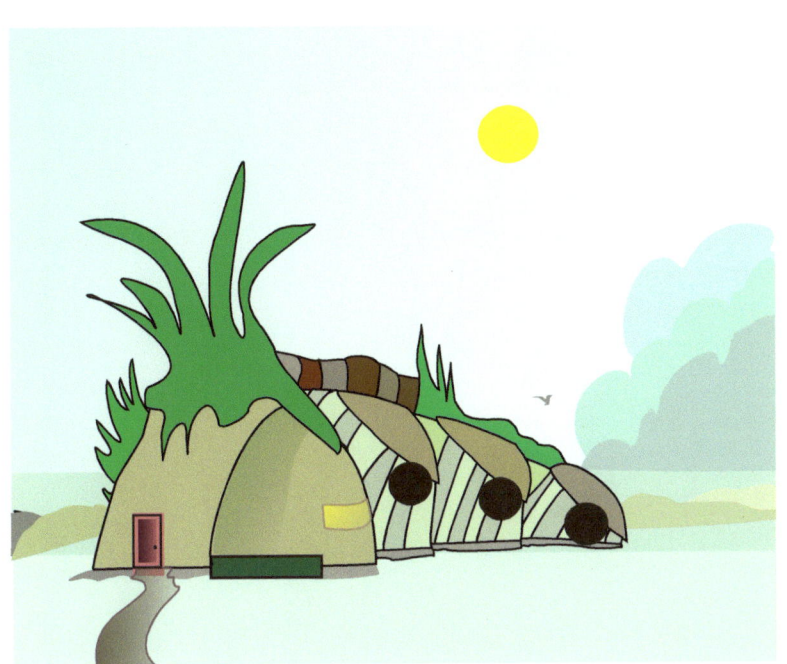

Random Spatterings

Sometimes there could be more than there is.
Sometimes I know you're a better man than I
as most men are.
The solitude of the night can be a comfort:
the wind on my back, the jacket around me.
I have told many stories about this and that.
Good people have thought me good.
Am I just a trickster?

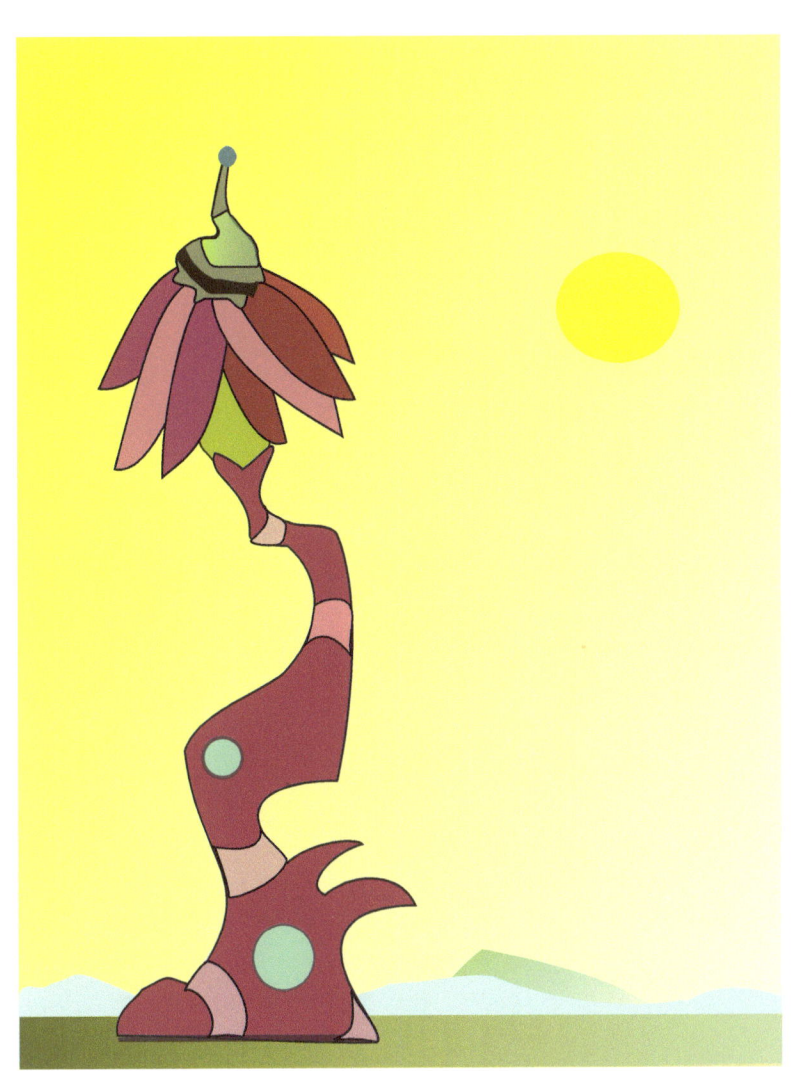

Fragment

Feeling the drizzle
seeing shadows
where fear comes from

Knowing the reason
is no cure
only illusion

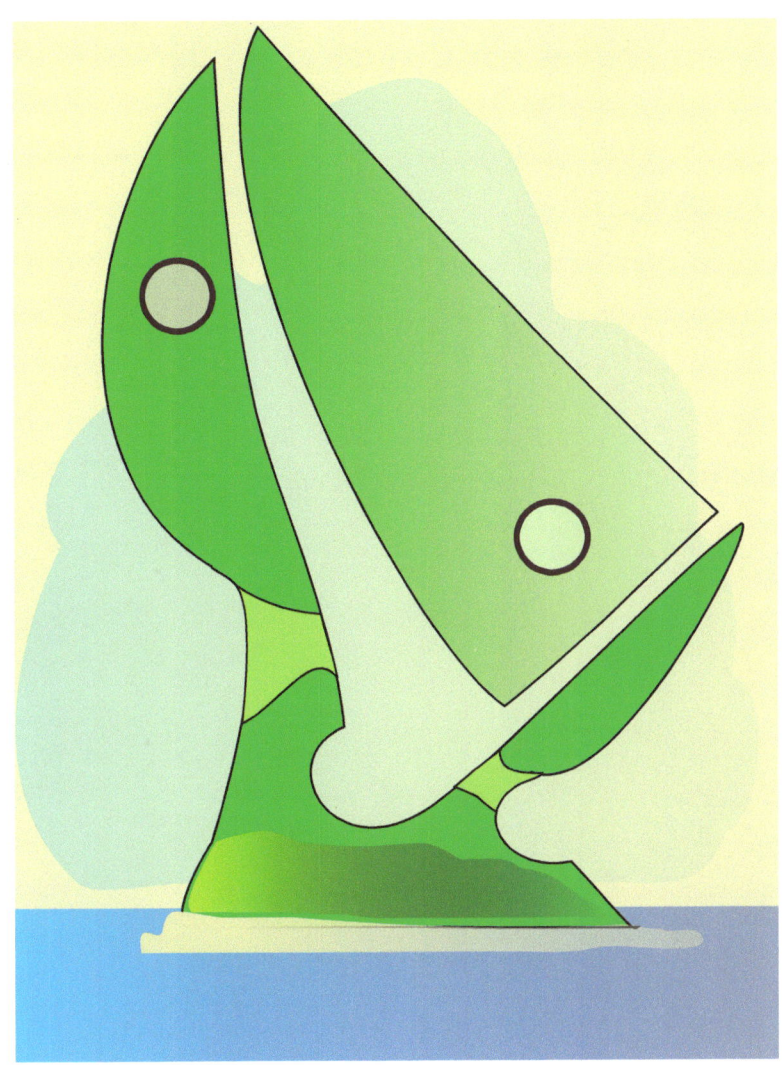

The Art
For Steven D. Larson

Traveling through
Running light
Caught in colors
Asked for truth
Yes it could be
The same for me

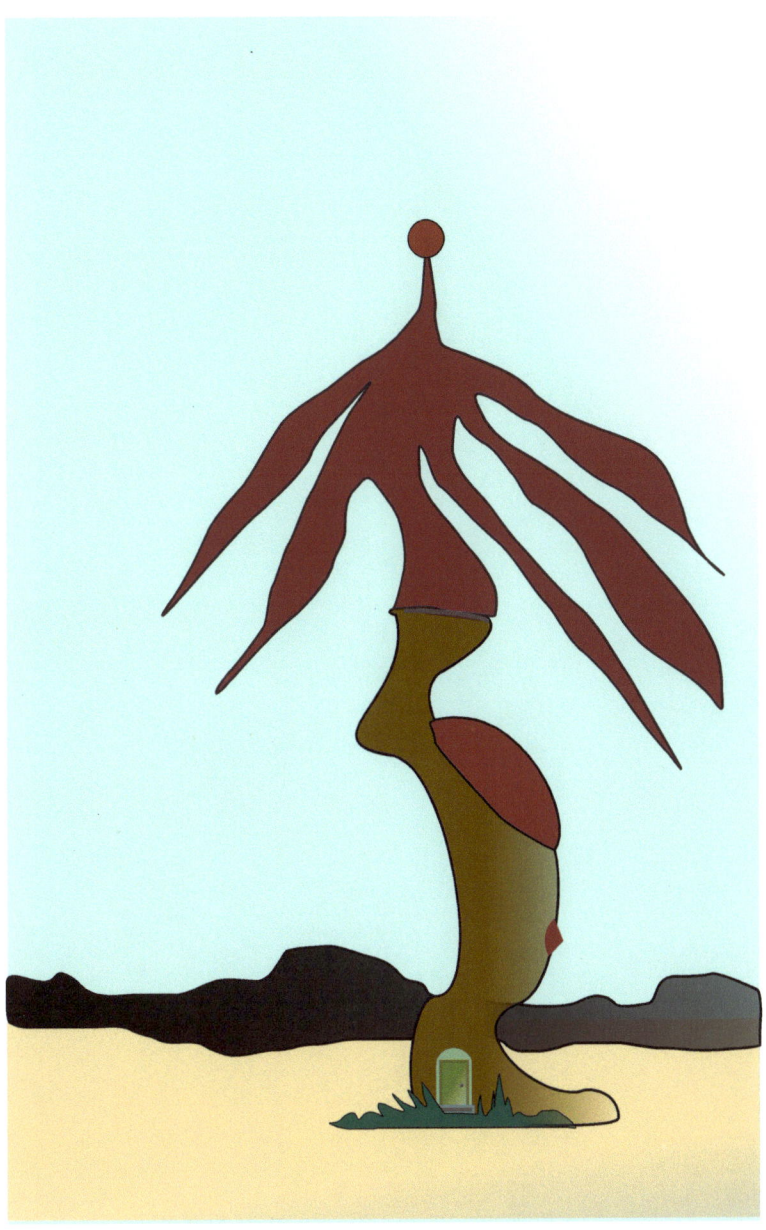

On A Gallery Wall

Yellow between green and blue
Green next to blue after yellow
Orange creeps in

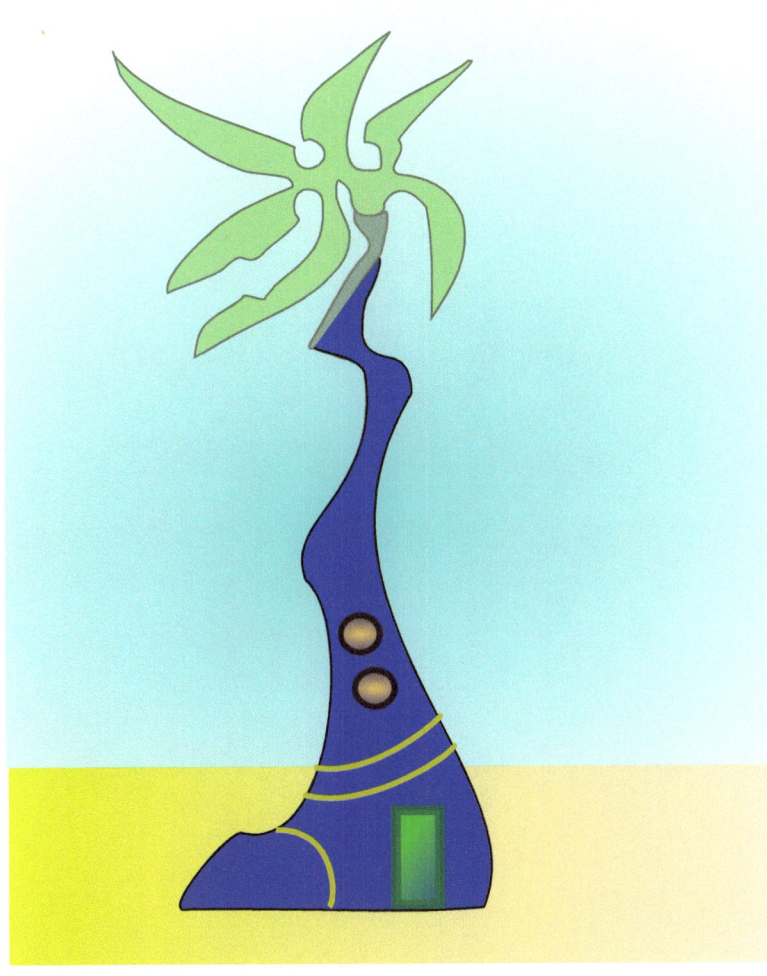

Into the Vast

The dream came and left
a mark on the fools
What town is this one asked
hoping for easy revelation
It doesn't look like here
but it is
Oh, there's a blue door

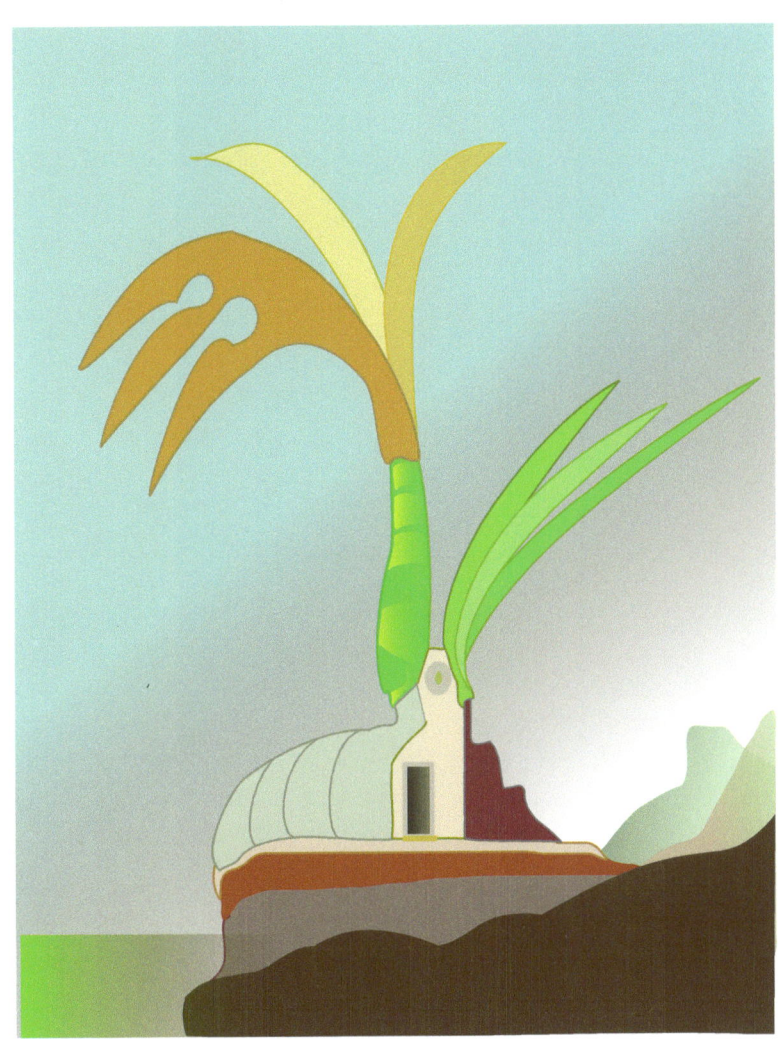

A Soliloquy of Peace

It darkens outside
Here
Inside a glow
From your mind

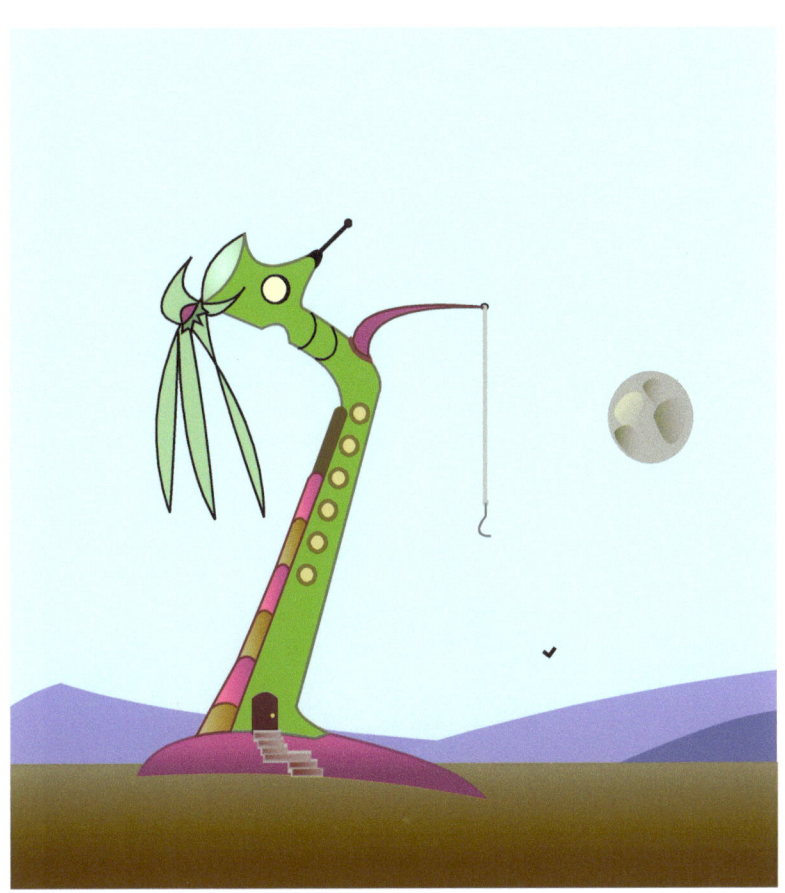

Notes On Blue

The color not the feeling
informs the mind
of coming brightness

The feeling not the color
drives the perception
to wonder

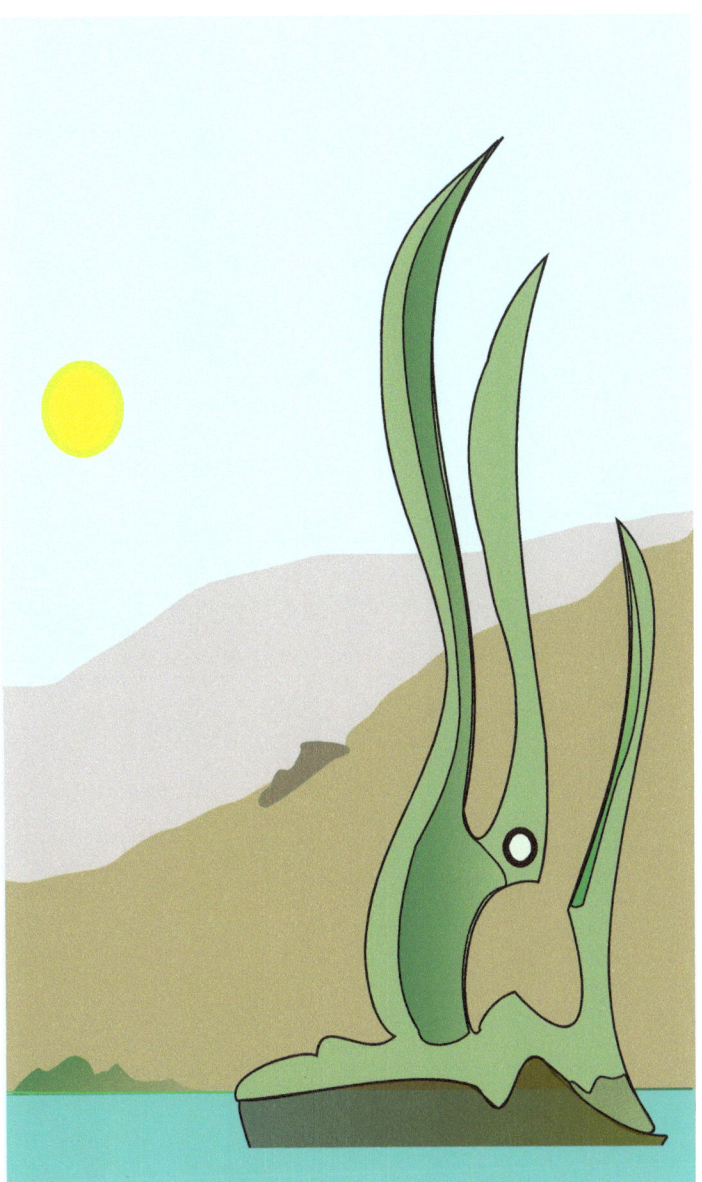

The Monastic Shower

Coming clean
in more ways than known.
Looking deep and through.
Spooked.

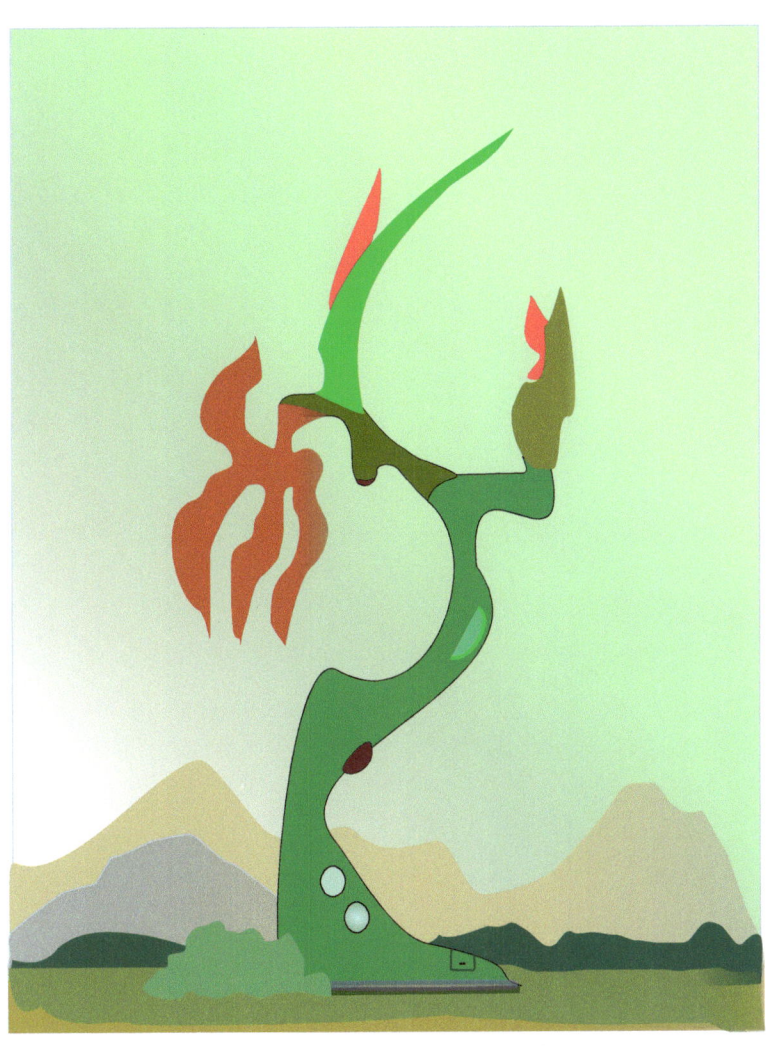

Sitting here is a challenge
to myself

To see how much fun I can have
or how long I can sit alone

It's always a test
Makes me tired to think of it

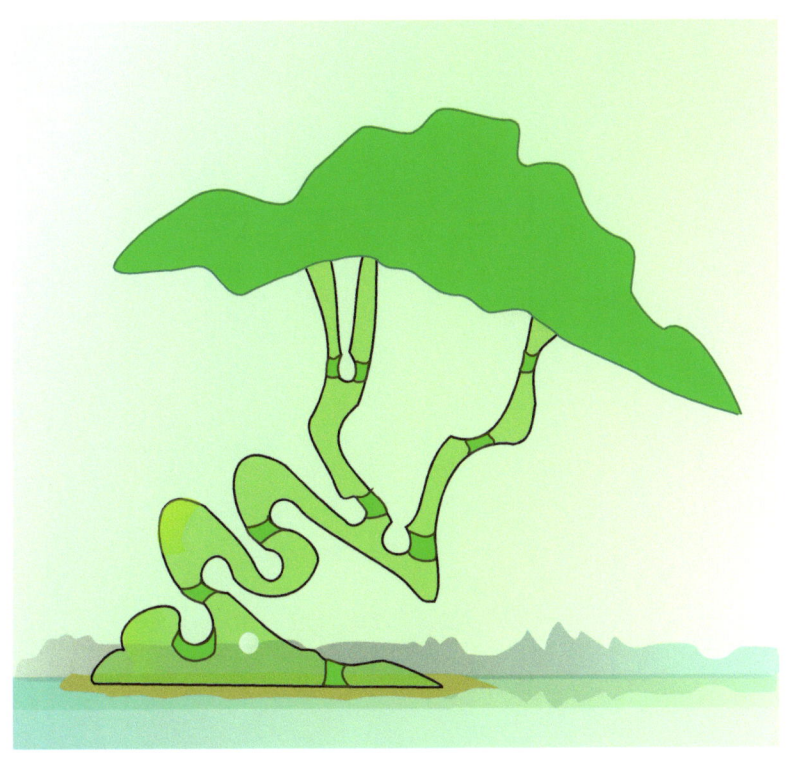

Roads

I drove by your house
last night
on my way somewhere
Your place was dark
and I got somewhere

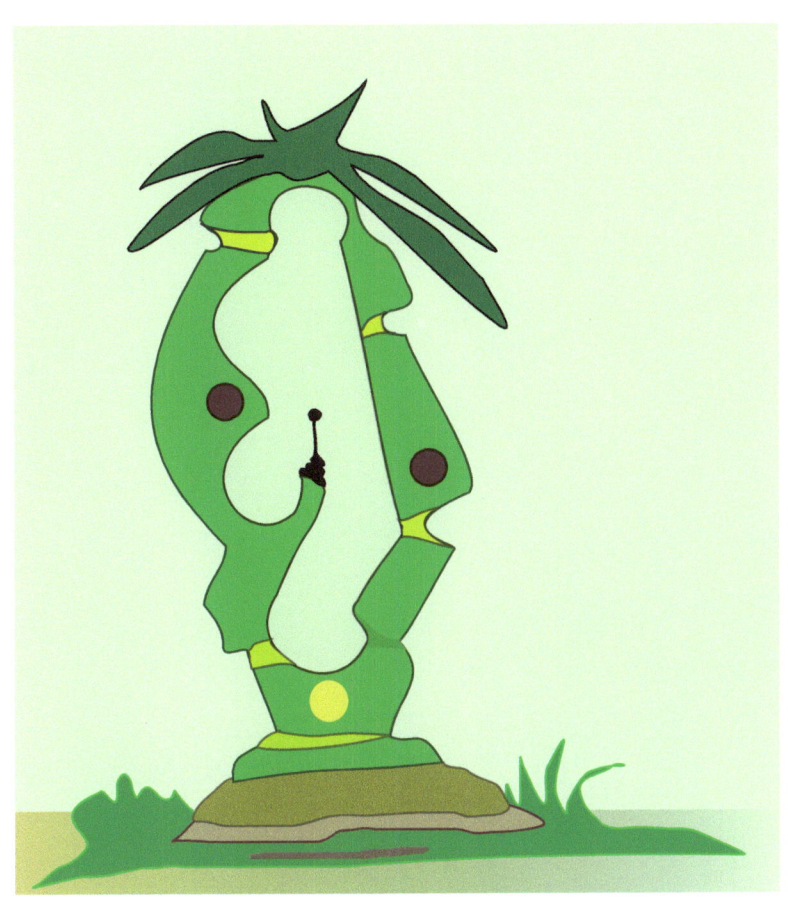

On A Stool

I'm waiting for a thought
to come
maybe through the window
or from the left side of the room

The bearer could be the wind
The door is open

A noise
tells of flurries
of choices

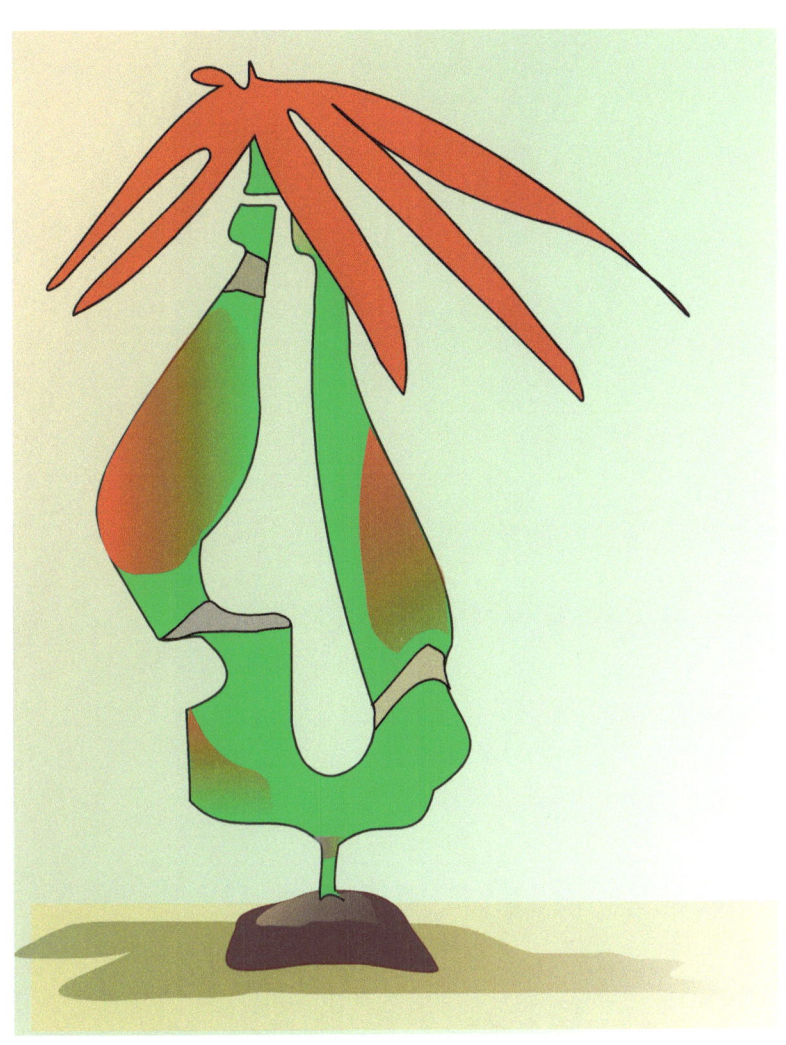

Could write a poem about nothing
It would be
Bigger than nothing itself

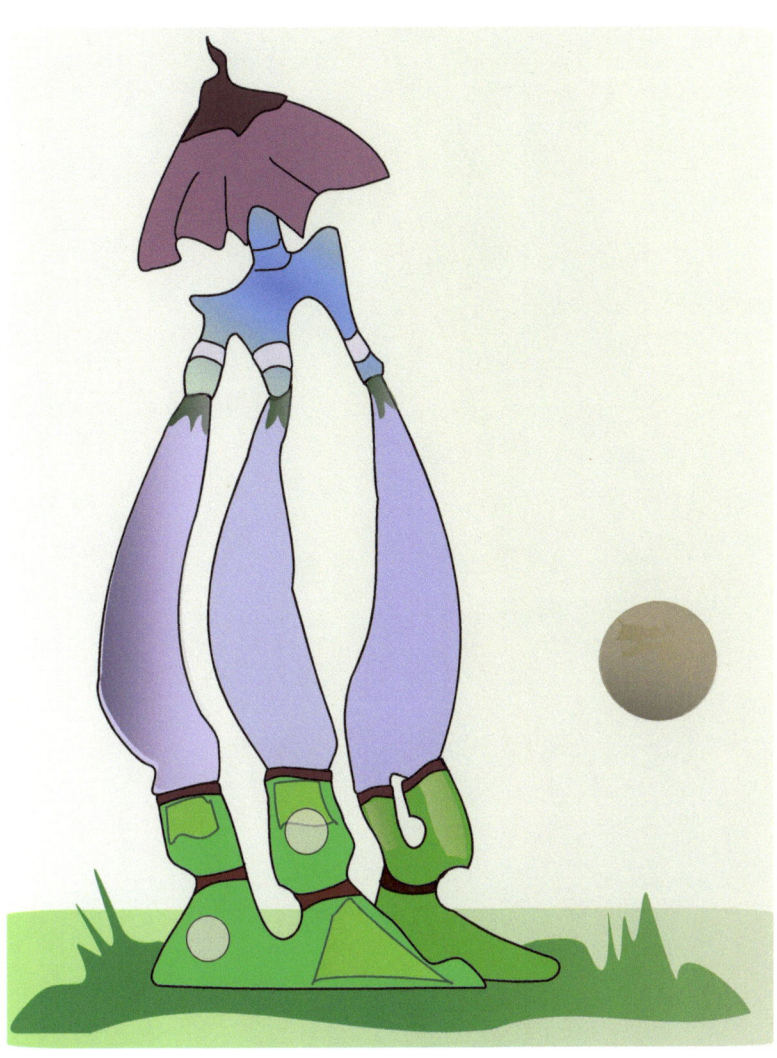

The Beautiful Misty Day

Here waiting   there waiting
Each at a different place
Now looking at the girls at the next table
Seemingly dark but fun
Wondering how you missed being here
Instead you're there away for awhile
Long time   short time
Hope is anytime

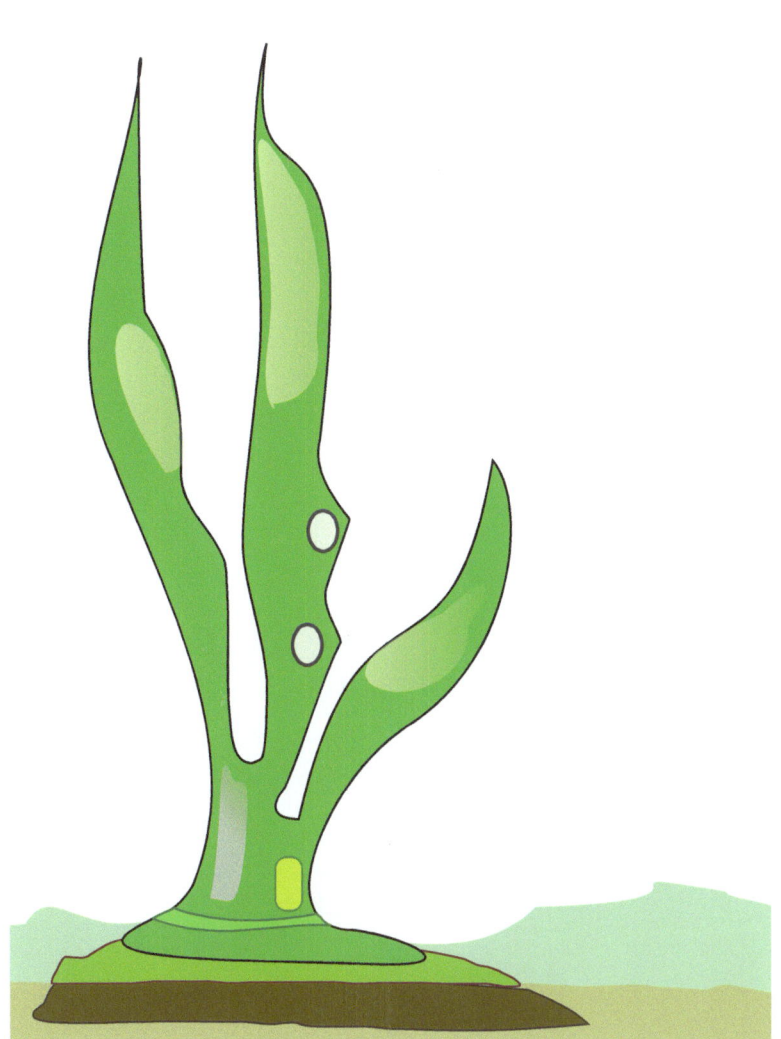

The black walnut lying on the ground
does not make a sound.
A trotting dog kicks it into some leaves
by whom will it be found?

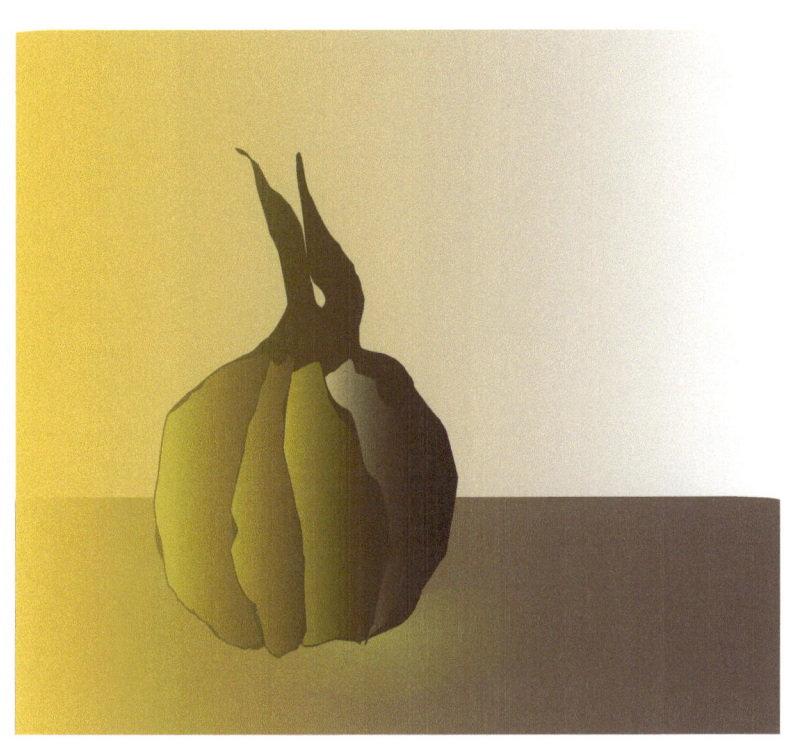

Epistle from the Park

Telescopic views turn microscopic
in the mind's storm.
Quickly a dog runs by
holding a packet of good deeds
that children hope to play forever.
Pretty letters and yellow dresses
describe the afternoon.
Hope never leaves here.
Breezes and dandelions summon.
Come here!
Then what?
The sun sets and it gets loud.

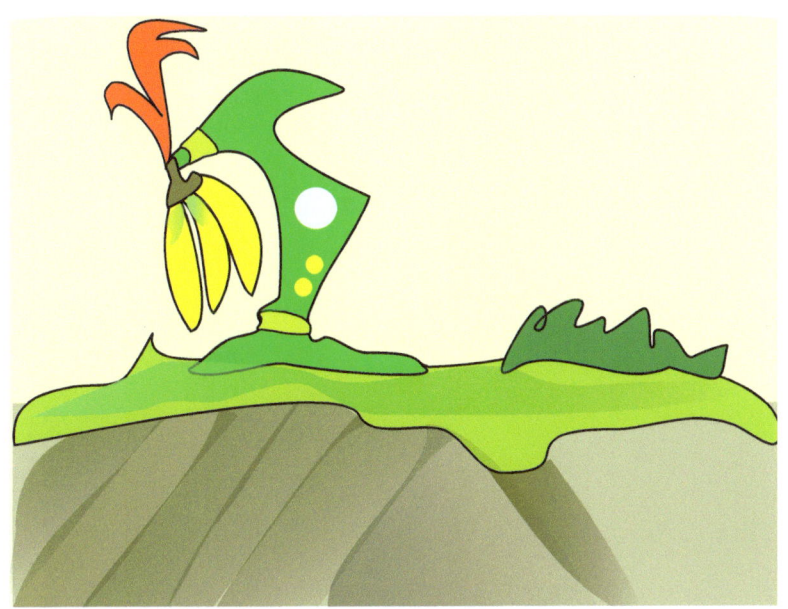

One Total

Can't read any longer
without falling asleep it seems.
Am I that tired?
Been to the woods, the river.
Been down roads.
Can't help what was done,
but was there it seems.
Echoes abound in the car,
penetrate the mind.
Perplexing it seems.
Get down the joyous track.
Get up to blow holes.
Free the dream to expand.
Learn what was not yet real.
Control the thought, then focus.
But no help here it seems.
This is nothing more
or less to converse about
it seems.

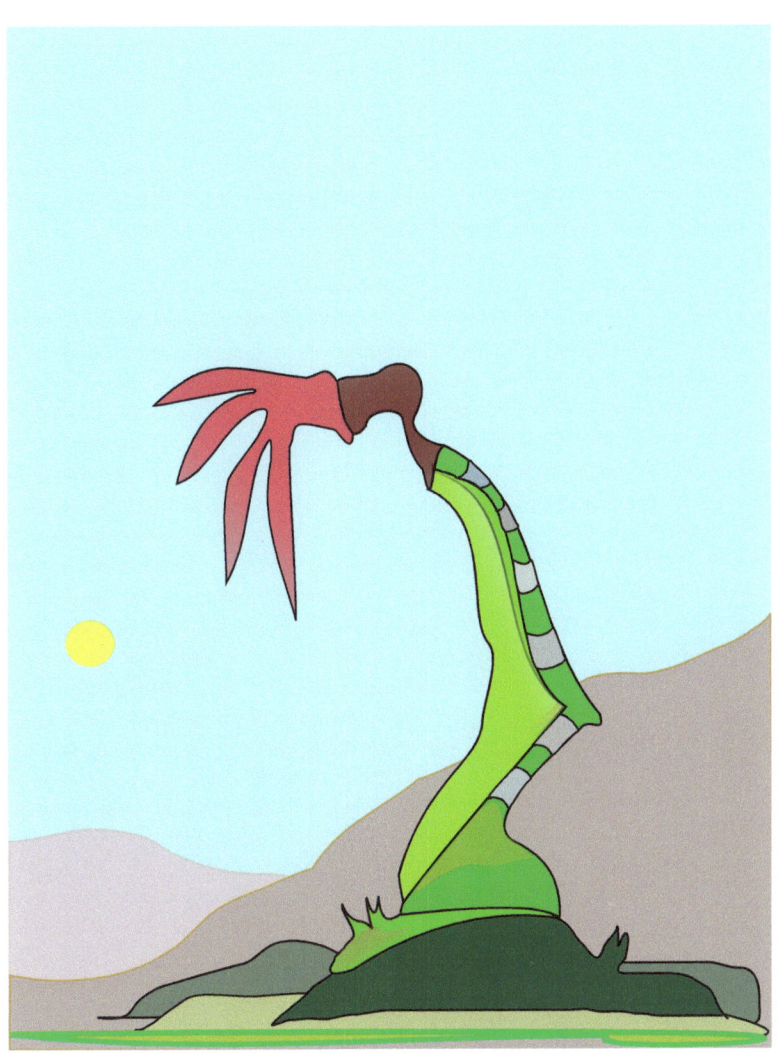

Poem 63

Hold tears
as
sweet water
in
small hands

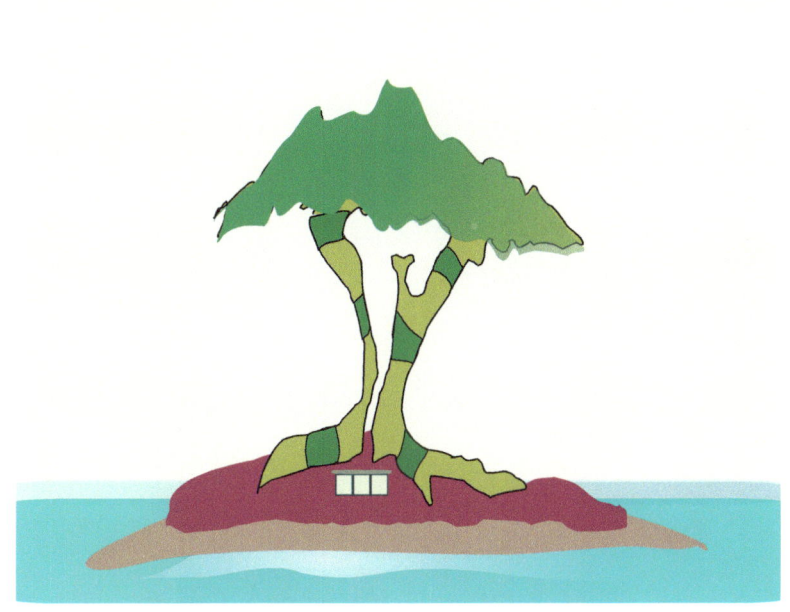

Page The Seventh

The day is already old
A man believes himself
He thinks he's an ogre
Crusty toes suggest it
Dirty briefs prove it
Quiet
Then she knocks on the door
He creeps to the basement
Quiet
For a long time

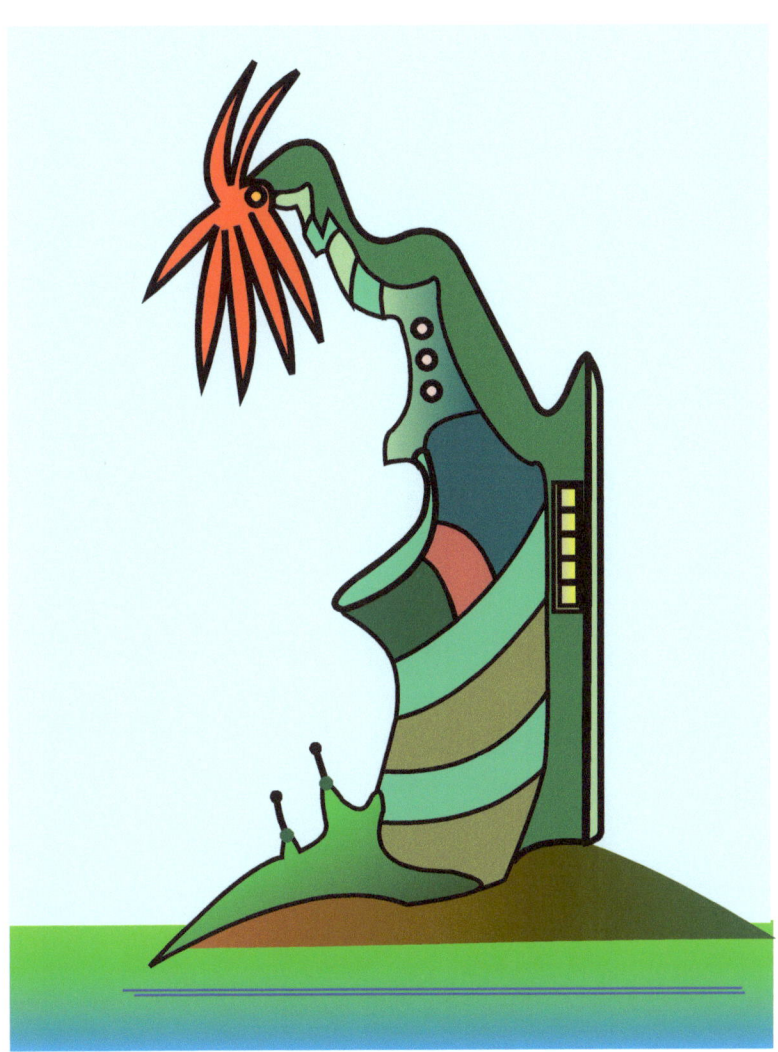

I do not know where I am: this space,
        place I'm wandering.
The friends and idiots I left behind;
        the fools and geniuses I'll meet ahead,
they could all tell stories.
The future is death; the future is light.
The two mix well, but not entirely.

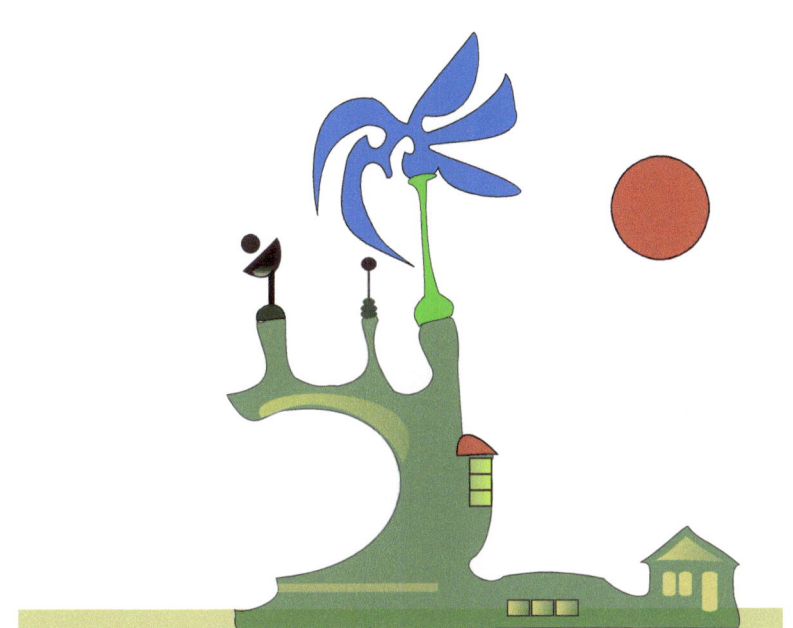

To The Trippers Moving

The eco-plastic wares forever,
and the water smells funny at this dump.
The rock'n'roll radio helps propel thoughtful fools
to the destination marked in chalk.
It can't be said out loud easily,
but the long word's syllables
render rhythm to the image of
her back side in front of a dark curtain.
They don't know where they've been.
Where they go is uncertain,
but arrival is now.
A rusty Buick departs.

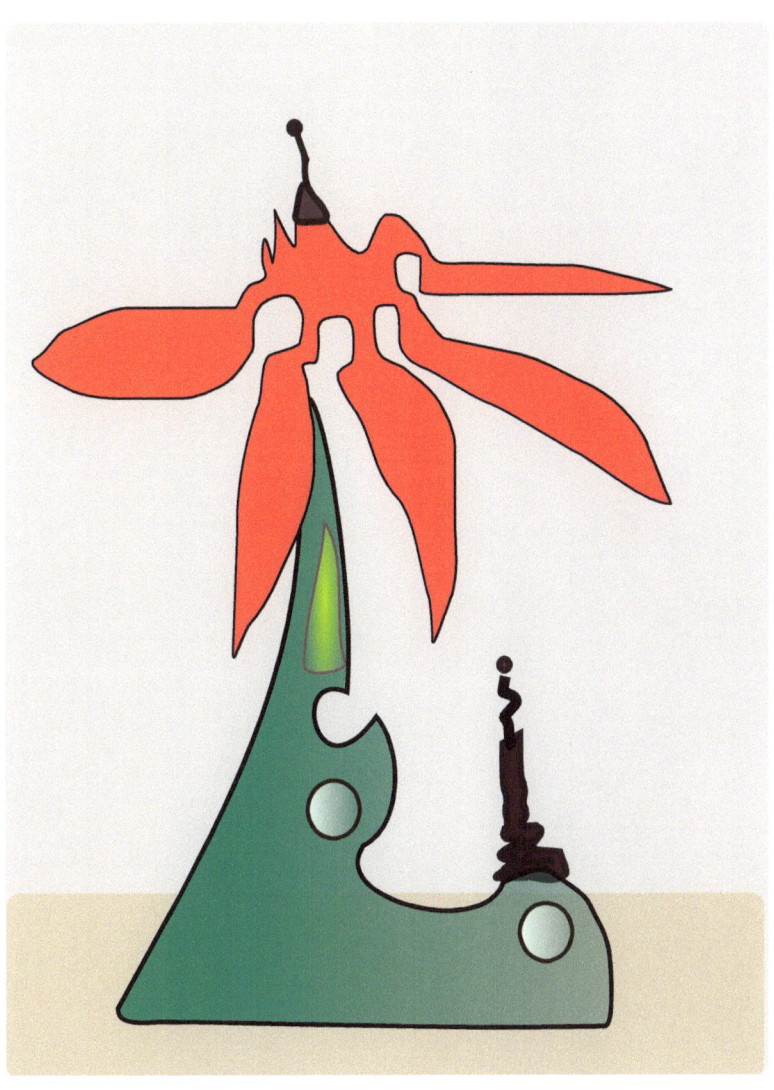

Spoke of the wind
to the crowd
in the mirror
No one moved

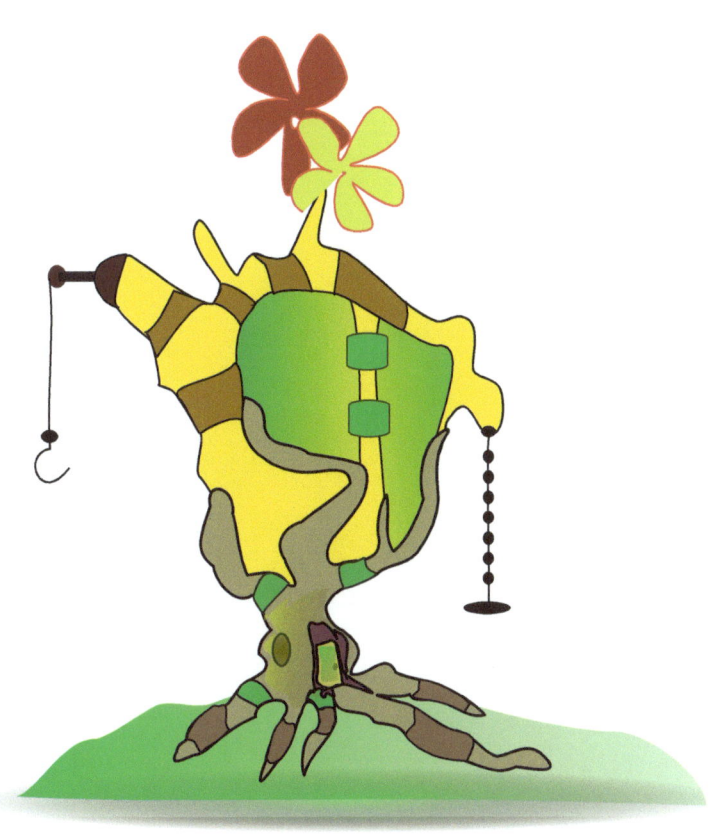

Open

Door
window
then roof

    Cold
    apartment
    and patio

Hot
stove
and ideas

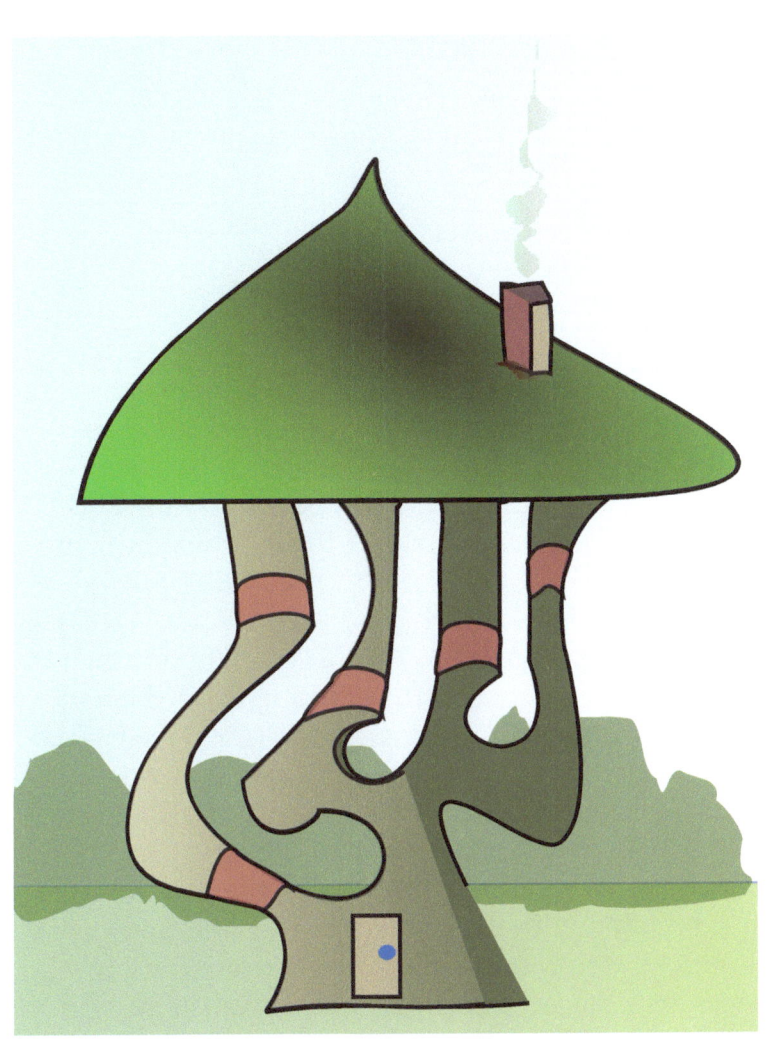

About the Author and Artist

Charles Luden has been writing poetry for many years and is noted for giving entertaining readings sometimes with a jazz band. His work is both serious and at times humorous and can be found in FROM *THE LONELY COLD* (2009: Scurfpea Publishing) and in *VIRGIN DEATH* (1977), *WEST OF VENUS: Punk Love Poems* (1986), and chapbooks *THE POET ALONE* (1990) and *LE BOMB HYDRO* (2003) all published by Astro Black Books. From 1996 through 2001 he had a column entitled "The Fringe of Literary Decency" in the biweekly Sioux Falls *TEMPEST* independent paper which featured his poems. He is also a drummer and has been in several bands most notably No Direction, Exploding Parakeet, and Habitual Groove of It. He is an experimenter in the visual arts. Charles holds a B.A. in biology from Augustana College, Sioux Falls. In his career he has been a chemist, leather craftsman, and co-founder of Ernie November stores. He was awarded the 2004 Sioux Falls Mayor's Award in Literary Arts. Charles' books and CDs are available through Scurfpea Publishing.

Boyd McPeek has been a farm boy, a SD School of Mines graduate with a commission in the Corp of Engineers, an insurance professional, a captain in the Army reserve, safety director for a Sioux Falls manufacturing company, unemployed, under-employed, a consultant, a programmer and now a process analyst for a financial services company. Throw in a love of science fiction, wildlife and gardening and you have the inspiration for his work. He has filled sketchbooks with doodles and his basement with wood sculptures. But it was only in the last 10 years that he has started to sell his work in galleries. Finding a computer language that let him turn his doodles into art was the outlet he needed for his creative instincts to blossom. His work is available from: Piper Fine Art Gallery (www.pipercustomframing.com) and Eastbank Art Gallery (eastbankartgallery.com), both in Sioux Falls, SD.

68

Book design by Steve Boint.
Thanks to Nancy Dickinson for grammatical assistance.
The font is ITC Giovanni Book.
Summer 2010